ACTIVISTS ASSEMBLE

WE ARE ALL EQUAL!

SHANNON WEBER · JADE ORLANDO

KINGFISHER
LONDON & NEW YORK

For all children who
have been made to feel like they're
inferior or don't belong. You are precious
and needed in this world.—S.W.

For those with the courage
to make a difference—J.O.

Copyright © Macmillan Publishers International Ltd 2021
First published 2021 in the United States by Kingfisher
120 Broadway, New York, NY 10271
Kingfisher is an imprint of Macmillan Children's Books, London
All rights reserved.

Text copyright © Macmillan Publishers International Ltd 2021
Illustration copyright © Jade Orlando 2021

ISBN 978-0-7534-7693-2 (HB)
978-0-7534-7692-5 (PB)

Distributed in the U.S. and Canada by Macmillan,
120 Broadway, New York, NY 10271

Library of Congress Cataloging-in-Publication data has been applied for.

Senior editor: Catherine Brereton
Senior designer: Laura Hall

Kingfisher Books are available for special promotions and premiums.
For details contact:
Special Markets Department, Macmillan
120 Broadway, New York, NY 10271.

For more information please visit:
www.kingfisherbooks.com

Printed in China
2 4 6 8 9 7 5 3 1
1TR/1020/UG/WKT/128MA

CONTENTS

What is Equality?   4

GENDER
What is Gender?   6
Fighting Gender Stereotypes   7
Understanding Feminism   8
Feminism for Boys and Men   9
Girls' and Women's Rights Around the Globe   10
Fighting Beauty Myths   12

SEXUALITY
What is Sexuality?   14
Activism for LGBTQ+ Rights   16

DISABILITY
What is Disability?   18
Disability and Inequality   20

RACE
What is Racism?   22
The Legacy of Slavery   24
Apartheid   26
Colorism   28
Black Lives Matter   30

CLASS
What is Classism?   32
Workers and Trade Unions   34
Fighting Worker Exploitation   36

NATIONALISM
What is Nationalism?   38
Understanding Xenophobia   39
Equality for Immigrants and Refugees   40

RELIGION
What is Freedom of Religion?   42
Religious Pluralism   44
Religion and Equality   45

Glossary   46
Index   48

ACTIVITIES
Discussion Time   49
Quiz   55
Find Out   57
Get Active   59
Writing and Drawing Activities   61

WHAT is EQUALITY?

Equality is when everyone is treated with respect and kindness. It is when they are able to have the same opportunities, which includes equal access to resources such as food, shelter, physical safety, education, healthcare, and good jobs. In an equal world, everyone would be able to be themselves, to have their differences honored while living in peace. Everyone would be treated fairly and would be able to make the best of their lives.

Sadly, we do not live in a world of equality. Due to forms of oppression such as racism, sexism, ableism, homophobia, transphobia, xenophobia, and more, many people face enormous challenges in being able to live their best lives. On the other hand, those who have privileges, such as being born into a wealthy family, benefit from inequality. Some people have far more resources than others and are treated extra well in society, which often makes them think inequality isn't a big deal. They may even think that they'll suffer if other people gain more rights. But in reality, equality makes life better for everyone.

It's important to remember that inequality didn't come out of nowhere—it has a long and complex history. To understand how society came to be so unequal, we must learn about the injustices that have built up over time. We have to study and listen to those who have been fighting inequality for generations if we're going to make things better.

People who take action to achieve equality are called activists. In this book we'll learn about many kinds of activism and famous activists around the world, from kids fighting for climate justice and girls' education to the inspiring courage of the Black Lives Matter movement.

Will you take action for equality and become an activist, too?

WHAT is GENDER?

We can think about gender as a collection of traits, styles, and meanings that we associate with being masculine or feminine and male or female. For example, dresses are usually associated with femininity, girls, and women. Societies make a lot of predictions about how a person will act and what their interests will be based on gender.

Gender is often wrongly thought to be the same as a person's physical sex. In other words, people with penises are called boys or men and are assumed to like masculine things, while people with vaginas are called girls or women and are assumed to like feminine things. But gender goes beyond our bodies—it's about what we like and prefer, what makes us happy in our hearts, minds, and souls. There are feminine boys, masculine girls, people who express themselves in ways that are both feminine and masculine, and also nonbinary people, who don't identify as male or female. Gender is helpful to express who we are, but it shouldn't limit us or make us less than equal.

TRANSGENDER

Transgender, or trans, people are people whose gender is something other than the sex they were assigned at birth. For example, a doctor might call a baby male based on their body, but in the person's mind, heart, and soul they feel female. Trans people wrongly face much inequality and discrimination in society.

FIGHTING GENDER STEREOTYPES

Gender stereotypes are when people think certain things are only for boys or for girls. Societies are sexist, and things viewed as "for girls" (like shopping and make-up) are often seen as silly or less important. We may tell girls that they won't grow up to understand math and science as well as boys, discouraging them from pursuing careers in those fields. And we may tell boys that they're not allowed to cry, play with dolls, or like the color pink.

But did you know that in many places before the 1940s, baby boys were dressed in pink while baby girls were dressed in blue? We may think there are unchanging "rules" for gender, but the story is a lot more complicated. There's no "right" way to be any gender. We are all human beings, capable of expressing ourselves in the ways that feel right for us. Anything else promotes gender inequality.

Often there are sexist double standards when it comes to how people act; for example, a boy might be called confident or assertive, but a girl could act the same way and be criticized as bossy!

UNDERSTANDING FEMINISM

Feminism is activism for gender equality. While feminists want people to be treated equally regardless of gender, they particularly highlight how the way most societies work leads to continued inequality for girls and women.

Today's feminists fight for a wide range of rights. These include reproductive justice, which is the right to have or not have children; being free from violence and abuse; equal pay in the workplace; access to education at all levels; and affordable healthcare and childcare. Feminists also fight for equality for those women treated particularly unequally, such as women of color, poor and working-class women, immigrant women, LGBTQ+ women, and women with disabilities.

SUFFRAGETTES

The suffragettes were early 20th-century British and Irish feminists who used radical protest to push for women's right to vote. Their chief political group, the Women's Social and Political Union (WSPU), was founded in 1903 by Emmeline Pankhurst. Suffragettes chained themselves to buildings, yelled at government officials, destroyed property, and got arrested dozens of times. Emmeline once said, "[T]he condition of our sex is so deplorable that it is our duty to break the law in order to call attention to the reasons why we do." Some women in England, Wales, and Scotland gained the right to vote for the first time in 1918, and women there achieved full voting equality in 1928.

FEMINISM for BOYS and MEN

One way boys and men can help achieve gender equality is by doing an equal amount of chores around the house. This labor—which is most often unpaid—usually falls to girls and women.

Boys and men, too, are harmed by gender stereotypes. It's not healthy for boys to grow up thinking they shouldn't cry or talk about their emotions, for example. On the other hand, boys and men have male privilege, which is the unearned advantages they get in society just for being male. The more other forms of privilege a man has, such as white privilege and class privilege, the better he is treated in society and the fewer obstacles he faces in life.

Feminism asks boys and men to help build a world where girls and women are treated equally and can live their best lives. Gender equality makes things better for everyone—it's even been shown that countries with more gender equality have stronger economies!

In 2019, Finland, the world's 11th-richest country, hit the headlines when it appointed the world's youngest-ever female prime minister, Sanna Marin, aged 34. Some of the top ministers in her government were young women, too.

Girls' and Women's Rights Around the Globe

Women and girls around the world fight for the right to go to school, pursue whatever careers they wish, have economic equality with men, be safe from gender-based violence and sexual harassment, and be represented equally as leaders in government, among so many other issues. Their concerns and campaigns as activists may differ depending on which country or area they're in and how sexism affects their lives in different ways, but when it comes down to it, they're all fighting to be equal.

In 2015, women worldwide earned an average of only 60-75 percent of what men earned.

In 2020, only 21 of the world's 195 heads of government were women!

THE GENDER POVERTY GAP

Women and girls, despite making up over half the world's population, find themselves in high levels of poverty compared to men. Women are paid less than men and are often expected to do more childcare. What's more, in career fields dominated by women, such as teaching, workers are paid less money than in fields dominated by men. Feminists point out this inequality and think of ways to tackle it, with the aim of creating global economic justice for girls and women.

MALALA YOUSAFZAI (BORN 1997)

Do you know the youngest person to ever win a Nobel Peace Prize? If you answered **MALALA YOUSAFZAI**, you're right. In 2014, aged just 17, Malala won the award for her activism fighting for Pakistani girls' right to an education. From a young age, growing up in Pakistan, she spoke out for this right. One day Malala was targeted by the Taliban, a terrorist group that tried to ban girls from going to school where she lived. A Taliban gunman shot Malala, but she survived and kept speaking out! She spoke at the UN on her 16th birthday and published the book *I Am Malala*. Today she continues her activism, and has even opened a school for Syrian refugee girls in Lebanon. Malala's courage and tenacity show us how girls all over the world are assembling to fight for their freedom.

Fighting Beauty Myths

Because sexist societies place so much importance on girls and women being beautiful, girls grow up thinking that being pretty is one of the most important things they need to accomplish in life. This can make them feel bad about themselves while upholding oppressive, discriminatory ideas about what counts as beautiful.

Western beauty norms influence the rest of the world. They uphold the message that girls and women must be white, thin, feminine, and abled, among other attributes, to be beautiful. Girls and women who aren't these things may develop self-hatred and low self-esteem, and think they must buy weight-loss products or even surgically alter their bodies to try to become thinner and "prettier." This allows companies to make money from girls and women feeling horrible about their bodies.

Feminists, in contrast, fight back against these beauty myths. Feminists say that there are so many ways to be beautiful, and also, there are so many more important things to be than beautiful! They fight for a world where all girls and women can be proud of not only how they look, but also their intelligence, kindness, compassion, humor, and bravery.

WHAT is SEXUALITY?

Our sexuality is based on being sexually attracted to other people. We can be attracted to someone of a different gender, the same gender, more than one gender, or no one at all. The gender or genders a person is attracted to is called their sexual orientation. Many people know what their sexual orientation is when they're young, while others figure it out when they're older. All sexual orientations are valid, even though some people are treated unequally based on others' judgments about them.

SEXUAL EQUALITY AND LGBTQ+ RIGHTS

People want to be treated equally regardless of their sexual orientation. They also want the freedom to be able to express their sexuality, as long as they have consent and aren't harming anyone, and to form families with those they fall in love with. LGBTQ+ people (lesbian, gay, bisexual, transgender, and queer, with the plus sign representing some other identities) often experience homophobia (the fear and hatred of gay people) or transphobia (the fear and hatred of transgender people) in their daily lives. Many LGBTQ+ people around the world don't have equal rights under the law. Sometimes they are rejected by their families due to prejudice against their sexual orientation or gender. As we'll see, LGBTQ+ people and their friends and loved ones have been fighting for LGBTQ+ equality for decades.

CONSENT

Sexual equality relies on consent. Consent means—when you are old enough to do so—enthusiastically agreeing you want to do something sexual with someone, and knowing how to do it safely. It means you can stop at any time if you're not comfortable. No one should make you feel guilty or scared in order to do something sexual with you.

REPRODUCTIVE FREEDOM

For many people, a big part of being able to express their sexuality safely is knowing they have reproductive freedom. This means having control over whether you want to give birth to children or not. It means that people who don't want to, or aren't ready, have safe and affordable access to birth control and abortion. For people who do want to give birth, it means they have the support and resources needed to have a safe and affordable pregnancy and a good life with their future baby (healthcare, nutrition, safe shelter, parenting education, and childcare). Feminists have been protesting for reproductive freedom for over a hundred years.

Activism for LGBTQ+ Rights

In June 1969 in New York City, LGBTQ+ people were tired of being treated unequally. At the time, it was illegal for two men or two women to dance together in bars and clubs. Being gay was seen as wrong and bad, and gay people were fired from their jobs if anyone found out about their sexual orientation. At the Stonewall Inn, a gay bar in New York, the police would often barge in and make fun of customers, arrest and throw them in jail, and even assault them.

But on June 28 1969, the bar's customers fought back against the police, becoming activists for sexual equality in the process. They let the world know they were sick of homophobia and transphobia and that they had the right to live their best lives. These events became known as the Stonewall Rebellion, which helped pave the way for the modern gay rights movement. In honor of Stonewall and LGBTQ+ freedom, pride marches and parades are now held across the world every June. LGBTQ+ activists today continue to fight to be free from harassment and violence, stop youth bullying and homelessness, and make discrimination at work illegal, among other issues.

The rainbow became the symbol of LGBTQ+ equality in 1978 when Gilbert Baker designed the rainbow flag. The colors represent the diversity of LGBTQ+ people but also their unity as a group, fighting for equality and love.

EQUALITY FOR ALL FAMILIES

There are so many different kinds of families in the world! Some families include children, while others don't. Some have a mom, and some have a dad. Others have a mom and a dad, or two moms, or two dads, or grandparents raising the kids. Kids can have adoptive parents, step-parents, or both. There is no "right" way for families to look. Despite this, some families are treated unequally in society. Families with two moms or dads often face homophobia. Many have had to fight for decades for the right to get legally married and adopt children, and in many countries they still can't. If your parent or parents are LGBTQ+, you may have faced discrimination in school or elsewhere. But what really makes a family is love.

WHAT is DISABILITY?

Disabilities are physical, mental, or emotional differences a person has that can make it more difficult for them to thrive in societies that put the needs of abled (non-disabled) people first. When we talk about disability, most people think of physical disability, such as using a wheelchair or being blind or Deaf. But there are many types of disabilities, and not all are visible.

Discrimination against disabled people is called ableism.

NEURODIVERSITY

The different ways our brains work, help us process information, and respond to our environments is called neurodiversity. In daily life this may mean having different ways of learning, expressing moods, and reacting to highly stimulating situations, such as places with lots of noise and bright lights. Examples of neurodiversity include autism, ADHD, and dyslexia. Not everybody's brains work the same way, and that's okay! One way neurodiverse people have fought for equality is by getting some supermarkets to introduce time slots for autistic shoppers and their families, where the lights are dimmed and the music is lowered.

MENTAL ILLNESS

When we experience trauma and stress, that can harm our minds and emotions and cause mental illness. Examples of mental illness include depression, anxiety, and schizophrenia. Because it's our feelings getting broken instead of, say, an arm or a leg, many people don't think mental illness is real. But it is! This is why we must be mindful to include mental illness in our fight for disability equality.

GRETA THUNBERG (BORN 2003)

Swedish activist **GRETA THUNBERG** is known for her urgent calls to world leaders to save the planet from environmental destruction before it's too late. After learning about climate change when she was 8, she started protesting at her school at 15. This ignited worldwide attention. Greta, who is autistic, agrees that her neurodiversity helps her fight for justice because of how it shapes her view of the world. She has said, "I'm sometimes a bit different from the norm. And—given the right circumstances—being different is a superpower."

DISABILITY and INEQUALITY

Disabled people face high levels of poverty compared with others. Sometimes their disabilities prevent them from working, which means they don't have the money they need to survive. Other times their bosses don't accommodate their needs at work, or they can't find jobs because of ableism. Meanwhile, governments don't allocate enough resources to disabled people. When disabled people cannot access the things they need to fully engage in the world, their lives are deeply unequal.

DISABILITY ACTIVISM

Historically, disabled people have been denied the chance to speak for themselves about their lives and pursue their dreams. They've often been judged as inferior, pitied and talked down to, and even seen as having less valuable lives. Despite this, disabled people have always been speaking out, fighting for justice, as well as contributing so much to our world.

One way disabled people seek justice is through fighting for accessibility. This means making sure everyone can move around in the world, enter the same spaces, and fully participate in society. It means making sure that the environments we build around us, and our events and gatherings, are thoughtful and inclusive of all bodies and what those bodies can do. For example, we can make sure events are held in buildings with ramps and elevators so people who use wheelchairs and scooters can attend. Disabled and abled people must work together to create a disability-friendly world.

Access to healthcare is one of the most urgent needs of disabled people and one of the most important goals of disability activists. It means access to doctors, medicines, surgeries, equipment to do daily tasks and errands, service animals, therapists, psychiatrists, and more. All of these things can be expensive.

FRIDA KAHLO (1907-1954)

The artist **FRIDA KAHLO** was born in Mexico in 1907. After a bus accident in 1925, Frida became physically disabled and suffered extreme pain for the rest of her life. She used her bold, colorful paintings to explore many of the things she dealt with, such as her husband abusing her and being a bisexual woman in a homophobic, sexist society. Although she spent much time in bed, Frida fought for her right to artistic expression and expressed radical political views in support of oppressed people.

WHAT is RACISM?

Racism is discrimination against people of color due to negative beliefs about their racial background. Racism is based on prejudice plus power. It's upheld by people with racial prejudice who have the power to enforce this prejudice across a whole society.

To achieve equality, white people must understand how they benefit in society at the expense of people of color. This means understanding that even if a white person isn't trying to be racist, they still benefit from racism due to white privilege. It's white people's responsibility to stand up to this. This can be accomplished by listening to the needs and experiences of people of color, joining in anti-racist activism, and giving back to communities still suffering from the impacts of generations of slavery, colonialism, genocide, and legal discrimination.

UNDERSTANDING WHITE PRIVILEGE

White privilege is a term used to understand the unearned advantages white people get in society simply for having been born white. This privilege extends from everyday examples, such as being able to find bandages at the grocery store that match your skin color, to being paid more money for the same job and being overrepresented in media and government.

In 2013, nine-year-old Chicago boy Asean Johnson was the youngest speaker at the "Realize the Dream" rally commemorating the 50th anniversary of Martin Luther King, Jr.'s March on Washington. Asean spoke against the budget cuts and school closures harming Black and Latinx neighborhoods in Chicago. He saved his school from closing, and plans to run for mayor in 2025!

WHAT IS WHITE SUPREMACY?

White supremacy is when white people wrongly believe they're better than people of color and commit harmful actions to ensure they remain on top. When we think of white supremacy, we may think of terrorism like the Ku Klux Klan (KKK). But white supremacy is even bigger than a group like the KKK: it's a central way racial inequality has been established and maintained around the world.

White supremacy is how white people were able to think it was okay for them to capture and enslave millions of African people. It provided justification for invading dozens of countries and committing colonial violence and genocide. It's what helped countries in western Europe and North America emerge as powerful and wealthy while sapping the labor and natural resources of people of color. Understanding the history and legacy of white supremacy enables us to fight back against it for a just and equal future.

THE LEGACY of SLAVERY

Many people think that since the legal enslavement of Black, African, and Afro-Caribbean people ended more than 150 years ago, it has no connection to what's going on today. This couldn't be further from the truth. The historical violence inflicted on people of color reverberates into the present, as racial and economic inequality build up over generations.

Until 1865, Black families in the US, for example, weren't able to earn wages and buy property they could pass on to their children since they themselves were considered property. Even after slavery, Black Americans faced segregation laws known as Jim Crow laws, which restricted where they could live, find jobs, or vote as late as the mid-1960s. At the same time, white families generated centuries of wealth through enslavement, theft of indigenous land, and better treatment under the law. As a result, in 2016 the average white household in the US was almost ten times richer than the average Black household.

In 2015, Black filmmaker and activist Bree Newsome tore down a Confederate flag at the South Carolina state house. The Confederate flag was flown in the 1860s before and during the US Civil War, when 11 states tried to form their own country and keep enslaving Black people. Today, many white people want to keep flying this flag, even though it's considered a racist hate symbol that Black people typically find traumatizing and offensive.

In Haiti, Europeans began enslaving people starting with the arrival of Christopher Columbus in 1492. Enslaved Haitians successfully rose up against the French colonizers during the 1804 Haitian Revolution. After the revolution, however, France refused to recognize Haiti as a free nation unless Haitians paid the French for all the people France could no longer profit from as slaves. This put Haiti into extreme debt well into the 1940s. Haiti remains one of the poorest countries in the world, with human trafficking and modern slavery sadly widespread.

MODERN SLAVERY

As of 2016, more than 40 million people around the world are enslaved in some way. One in four enslaved people are children. People can be enslaved through being forced to work for little or no pay, through sexual abuse, through forced marriages, or a combination of all three. Enslavement can happen when someone is promised a new job in another country, for example, and then has their passport and money taken when they get there before being forced into a type of work they never agreed to. This is why migrants are particularly at risk, especially women and girls. Modern slavery happens all over the world.

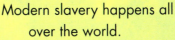

APARTHEID

South Africa has a history of European colonization. When Dutch colonizers arrived in the 1600s, many thought they were better than the African people who already lived there. In 1948, a racist political party called the South African National Party took over.

Under a policy called apartheid, which means "apart-ness," the white rulers made every aspect of society racially segregated. White people were treated better under "white laws", even though South Africa was overwhelmingly Black. By the 1950s, Black activists were organizing protests, with leaders such as Nelson Mandela. Activists were arrested, attacked, and even killed by white police officers. People around the world joined in the protest in the '70s and '80s as the violence continued. Then, in 1989, the activists won. Under a new constitution, Black people secured equal legal rights. In the 1994 election, Nelson Mandela was elected president and apartheid was dismantled.

EUGENICS

During the late 19th and early 20th centuries, eugenics was treated as a serious science. Eugenics is an attempt to "improve" the human race by encouraging certain groups to reproduce while limiting other groups from doing so. Scientists would do things like measure people's skulls and brains, claiming that white people had the biggest brains. Eugenics was a way for white people to uphold white supremacy by arguing that they were just "naturally" better and smarter than people of color. Later, eugenics was used by the Nazis to justify their genocide of Jewish people, disabled people, LGBTQ+ people, and other groups during the Holocaust. Today eugenics is rejected as unethical and as pseudoscience, which means something claiming to be scientific that actually isn't.

NELSON MANDELA (1918-2013)

NELSON MANDELA was a South African revolutionary and political leader who fought for 50 years against racism and apartheid. He was sent to prison in 1963, and sentenced for life the following year. He was in prison for 27 years in total until being freed in 1990. In 1993 he won the Nobel Peace Prize. The following year, the South African people elected him the first Black president of South Africa—the first election he was legally allowed to vote in. Nelson is known today as a hero who never backed down in the fight for equality despite the enormous toll it took on his life.

COLORISM

Due to the wide-ranging impact of racism and white supremacy, having light skin is valued in many parts of the world even among people of color. For example, light skin is prized in India and skin bleaching continues to be popular over 70 years after Indians won their independence from British rule. Discrimination against people with darker skin within communities of color is called colorism. Even though these communities don't have the white privilege that people of European ancestry do, there are still hierarchies and self-esteem struggles based on skin color. In an equal world, colorism wouldn't exist, and people of all skin tones would be equally valued and embraced.

Skin-lightening creams often contain dangerous chemicals. In 2015, creams containing these chemicals were banned in the West African country of Côte d'Ivoire.

Little Miss Flint (Born 2007)

AMARIYANNA "MARI" COPENY, known as Little Miss Flint, is a youth activist campaigning against environmental racism in her hometown of Flint, Michigan. She caught the attention of US President Barack Obama in 2016 when she wrote him a letter about the water crisis there at just eight years old. Since then, Little Miss Flint has protested against US President Donald Trump for failing in his promise to end the crisis. Her project Dear Flint Kids collects letters of support. She has also raised money for over 200,000 bottles of safe water.

ENVIRONMENTAL RACISM

Environmental racism is environmental injustice plus racism. It's the ways governments and companies pollute or damage the environment, often to make money, and do so in low-income communities of color. Activists against environmental racism say that their communities' lives and health are treated as less important than the lives of wealthy white people, who are far less likely to live in these polluted areas. Environmental racism is a global issue.

One example is US and Canadian governments building oil pipelines under indigenous land. These pipelines disrupt sacred sites and risk poisoning the water. Indigenous activists such as the Sioux tribe in Standing Rock, South Dakota protest against these actions. They declare, "Mni Wiconi!" or "Water is Life!". Meanwhile in Flint, Michigan, a majority Black and working-class US city, the city's water has been poisoned with lead since 2014. Despite an outcry from citizens, activism, and lead-related illnesses and deaths, the water is still contaminated.

BLACK LIVES MATTER

In 2013, Black US feminists Patrisse Cullors, Alicia Garza, and Opal Tometi created a movement called Black Lives Matter. The purpose of Black Lives Matter is to stand up for Black people's inherent worth, dignity, and right to safety in the face of an ongoing crisis of US police harassing, shooting, and killing unarmed Black men, women, and even children.

Black Lives Matter activists are everyday people in US cities—and cities around the world—who care about racial justice. They want Black children to be able to grow up in a nation where they don't have to be scared of racial profiling or the police. Racial profiling is a practice where certain groups of people of color are stopped more often by the police and accused of being criminals because of racist stereotypes. Black Lives Matter, like so many civil rights movements before it, fights for a future where racial equality is a reality, not just a dream.

Sometimes white people, who don't have to experience anti-Black racism firsthand, argue against the message of Black Lives Matter by saying, "All lives matter!" But while this is true, it's Black people in particular who are under attack from racism. Equality isn't always about treating people the same—sometimes it's about recognizing that different groups have different problems and need their suffering addressed in particular way.

STRENGTH IN DIVERSITY

As we can see, there are so many examples of how white supremacy has promoted racial inequality and profoundly harmed people's lives. But as we can also see, as long as there has been inequality, there have been people working for equality. There have always been people speaking out and assembling in acts of great courage, planning the activism needed to change the world for the better!

An important lesson for achieving racial equality, and all forms of equality, is the knowledge that our diversity is our strength. What does this mean? It means accepting the fact that humans can be different from each other without having to label one group as better than another. It means embracing our differences and celebrating the different perspectives and experiences we bring with us. How boring life would be if we were all the same! Each person and community has worth and value. Together we shine.

WHAT is CLASSISM?

When we think about equality, one of the most important factors is how much money a person has and the resources they have access to—food, education, housing, healthcare and more. When poor and working-class people are treated as less important or worthy of respect and resources than those with more money and from a higher social class, that's called classism. Classism is used as a weapon against poorer people, who may be told they don't deserve better lives because they're "lazy," "didn't work hard enough," or because that's simply "how it is." Wherever there is classism, there is inequality.

There is inequality when workers are paid low wages, cannot afford the healthcare they need, or go hungry in countries filled with wealth and food. In an equal world, everyone would have enough money to provide good lives for themselves and their families. No one would end up homeless. No one would be scared to go to the doctor because of how much it would cost them. And no one would be made to feel like they should be ashamed because of how much money they have, what kind of house they live in, or what kind of job they have.

EQUALITY OF OPPORTUNITY

Even though everyone should be treated equally, we aren't born into equal situations with equal opportunities. Some people are born into families, communities, or societies where they have very little, while others are privileged enough to have every advantage. For example, a girl who grows up in a poor or working-class family will typically face more obstacles in studying to become a doctor than a girl born to a wealthy family. She may not be able to afford study materials, may have to work an evening job that makes it harder to focus on schoolwork, or may be looked down on by wealthy peers and potential bosses based on the school or university she went to.

To understand what's stopping people from having equality of opportunity, we must also see how different forms of discrimination are connected. A working-class woman who makes less money doing the same job than her male co-worker, for instance, experiences both classism and sexism. It's the task of activists to work together to make equality of opportunity a reality.

Workers and Trade Unions

Improving the lives of workers is the focus of workers' rights activists, also called labor activists or trade union activists, who have been engaging in this struggle for generations.

A strike is when workers refuse to work until their bosses listen and take action.

The Industrial Revolution in the 17th and 18th centuries was built on the labor of workers who were underpaid and exploited. Many of them were immigrants, and many were children. Women were paid even lower wages than men. All worked long hours in dangerous conditions where it was common to experience serious injury and even death.

TRADE UNIONS

Trade unions were set up by workers who came together to demand better pay and conditions. Time and time again workers realized that if they all stood together, protested, and went on strike, they could force positive changes. After all, bosses can't make money without workers! Labor activism is why we have the concept of the weekend today. It's why we have set hourly limits on full-time work, a minimum wage, and workplace safety protections. As long as bosses exploit their workers for profit, trade unions will be needed. When workers believe in their own power and stick together, they can move mountains!

DOLORES HUERTA (BORN 1930) and CÉSAR CHÁVEZ (1927-1993)

In the US, migrant farm workers, many from Mexico, have long been exploited. They have been underpaid and exposed to dangerous working conditions as they pick fruit in the sun, sometimes without proper shade or water, while breathing in pesticides. Back in 1962, American labor activists **DOLORES HUERTA** and **CÉSAR CHÁVEZ** founded the National Farm Workers Association, which merged with another group to become the United Farm Workers of America. Dolores coined the motto, "¡Sí, se puede!", which means "Yes, it can be done!" in Spanish. The United Farm Workers empowered grape-farm workers to strike for better wages and safety protections, and organized boycotts. A boycott is when people protest by refusing to buy products that make money from harming workers or the environment. The idea is that if a company or government loses enough money, they'll be forced to make positive changes (even if they didn't care before).

US President Barack Obama (served 2009–2017) honored the farm workers' movement in his own campaign motto: "Yes we can!" This shows how different types of activism inspire each other.

FIGHTING WORKER EXPLOITATION

Even though there has been much progress since workers started organizing trade unions, there is still so much more to do. In the US, migrant farm workers are still exploited and their contributions continue to be undervalued, even though most Americans rely on these workers for their food. As workers in Western countries have won more rights, global clothing brands and other corporations exploit more people in poor countries where workers have weaker protections.

WORKERS ASSEMBLE!

Over the past decade, austerity measures have surged around the globe. These are the ways governments try to save money by cutting workers' pay and benefits, education funding, and other programs that help the most vulnerable people in society.

Workers all over the globe have been fighting austerity. Millions of people are taking to the streets, often risking their lives in the face of violent police forces or militaries to speak out against rising economic inequality. They demand their governments invest in higher-paying jobs, affordable healthcare and housing, and benefits for the most vulnerable, instead of hoarding wealth for those at the top of society. These protests are organized by trade unions and at the grassroots level, by groups of everyday people.

WHAT is NATIONALISM?

When people feel a strong connection to a nation, that is nationalism. It can be a way to celebrate what people enjoy about their country. However, nationalism becomes unequal and even dangerous when it makes people think their country's citizens are better or deserve better treatment than the citizens of other countries. Nationalism is often connected to racism, where people think only those from certain racial backgrounds "belong" in their country.

Nationalism can be deadly. In the 1930s and '40s, German dictator Adolf Hitler decided Jewish people—along with some other groups— didn't belong as "true" Germans. His Nazi party promoted this belief, and murdered millions of people. Whenever we hear that one country is better than the rest, or that only certain people belong in a country, we must ask, who is being excluded and hurt by these ideas?

SOPHIE SCHOLL (1921-1943)

SOPHIE SCHOLL was a teenager in Nazi Germany. When she got to college, she started questioning Hitler's ideas and joined a small anti-Nazi group called the White Rose. Sophie risked her life to write and give out pamphlets critical of the Nazis. But the Nazis found out and arrested her and the other White Rose members. Sophie was only 22 when the Nazis killed her. Today she is honored across Germany and the world for her incredible courage.

UNDERSTANDING XENOPHOBIA

Xenophobia (ZEN-o-FO-bee-uh) is a word that comes from the Greek "xenos," which means "stranger" or "foreigner," and "phobos," which means "fear." Xenophobia, then, is the fear or hatred of people considered "strange" or "foreign." It's used against anyone from a different country or seen as being from a different culture.

One example of xenophobia is a Muslim person in a country where Muslims are the minority being called a "terrorist" and told to "go back to where they came from." This act of hatred assumes that Muslim people must be from "somewhere else", that they don't belong in the place they live, and that they aren't welcome because they're (wrongly!) assumed to be scary or violent. Xenophobia relies on stereotypes and falsehoods to make it seem as if people in a group all think, look, or act the same. When we get to know each other and value how we're different but also part of the same human family, we can create a more equal future.

In the US, xenophobia was used to justify locking up Japanese-Americans in internment camps during World War II. It's currently being used to break apart and jail refugee families from Mexico and Central America trying to cross the border.

39

EQUALITY for immigrants and REFUGEES

Immigrants are people who migrate, or move, in to a new country. They do this for many reasons. Many hope for a better life for their families and want to earn more money. Some migrate for a new job or to study, while others fall in love and decide to move to their partner's country. There are almost 272 million immigrants worldwide.

Refugees, in contrast, are people forced to flee their homelands due to war, natural disaster, or persecution for their beliefs. For example, high numbers of refugees have fled to Europe due to the Syrian civil war and ongoing violence in Afghanistan, Iraq, and in several African nations. Many refugees face backlash in their adopted countries, where they're met with racism and xenophobia and find themselves in poverty. This is why the fight for equality must include immigrant and refugee rights.

Despite the obstacles they face, immigrants and refugees improve society. They can be found in every career, from harvesting food and cleaning buildings to inventing new technologies and saving lives as doctors. Wherever society has a need filled, there are usually immigrants and refugees to thank.

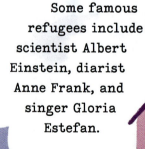

Some famous refugees include scientist Albert Einstein, diarist Anne Frank, and singer Gloria Estefan.

40

> Indigenous people south of the Arctic Circle in Canada are referred to as First Nations people in recognition of their original status.

EUROPEAN SETTLERS' IMPACT ON INDIGENOUS PEOPLE

In the Americas, Australia, and New Zealand from the 15th century, Europeans arrived with the goal of taking over and replacing the existing indigenous populations. This is called settler colonialism. Fueled by racism, nationalism, and xenophobia, Europeans committed genocide against the indigenous tribes. They felt entitled to the land, claiming it as "their" New World even though the tribes were the original inhabitants. Many of the Europeans were fleeing violence in their homelands, yet they went on to commit more violence against the people whose lands they invaded.

Indigenous people have always fought back against settler colonialism, however. They assert their right to control their land, water, and crops; gain access to good jobs and education; and celebrate and pass on their cultural traditions and spiritual beliefs. As they do so, they heal their hearts from the shame Europeans instilled in them over hundreds of years, replacing it with self-love and pride.

> The climate crisis is increasingly making people's homes unlivable around the world. This is driving the global migration of what are called "climate refugees."

41

WHAT is FREEDOM of RELIGION?

Freedom of religion is the right of all people to freely practice whatever religion—or no religion—they want. It sounds so simple, but the history of the world shows us that millions of people have been denied this basic form of equality, often violently.

RELIGIOUS WARS

Many wars have been fought in the name of one religious group against another. This includes different groups within the same religion fighting each other, as occurred during the Thirty Years War in 17th-century Europe between Protestant Christians and Catholic Christians. In the United States, the First Amendment to the Constitution guarantees freedom of religion.

FREEDOM FOR EVERYONE?

True religious freedom means that everyone's rights are protected equally. It means that no one is expected to follow a certain religion. It also means that minority religions—those that are smaller and less powerful in a society, such as Islam, Judaism, Hinduism, and Paganism in many Western countries—are treated the same as the dominant religions.

There are many places where religious freedom for minority religions is in danger today. Anti-Muslim violence is prevalent in India, in Myanmar against Rohingya Muslims (a minority ethnic group), and in the US through rising hate crimes against people perceived as Muslim since the September 11 2001 terrorist attacks and following the election of President Donald Trump.

> Religion is a system of beliefs about how our universe was made and what our purpose on this planet is. Most religions worship one or many gods and goddesses and have rules about right and wrong behavior.

ANNE HUTCHINSON (1591-1643)

ANNE HUTCHINSON was a Puritan woman who fought for religious freedom and was rejected by her community for it. Originally from England, Anne emigrated to the Massachusetts Bay Colony, where she became a preacher, midwife, and herbal healer. Many of her ideas challenged the views of the men who led her church, especially since they didn't think women should be equal religious leaders alongside men. As Anne gained followers, the men of her church decided to label her a heretic, which was someone who didn't listen to the Christian church and was seen as evil. They banished her and her family in 1637. The Hutchinsons traveled to Rhode Island, which was famous at that time for its religious freedom, and eventually New York. In her perseverance under persecution, Anne is remembered today as a champion for women's religious leadership and religious freedom.

Religious Pluralism

It is important for different religions to be able to coexist peacefully in a society. This is called religious pluralism. With religious pluralism, the diversity of the world's religions isn't seen as scary or bad. Instead, this diversity is seen as a way people can learn about each other and respect the freedom we all have to live our lives.

Religious pluralism is about making an effort to understand each other and recognize that despite our differences, humans share many important values in common. We all want to be loved. We want our lives to be meaningful. We want to feel safe and for our families to be safe. And we all deserve to be treated with respect and equality because we're here, right now, on this planet. Just as we don't all have to follow the same religion, we can do a better job of getting along with each other and valuing each other—whether we belong to a certain religion or no religion at all.

RELIGION and EQUALITY

When people are treated badly by others because of prejudice against their religion, that is religious discrimination. It can impact a person's ability to get and keep a job and home, and to access opportunities including education. It especially impacts people who belong to a minority religion in a society. Jewish people, for example, have faced religious discrimination for thousands of years, including being legally barred from certain jobs up through the 20th century and being subjected to extreme violence and terror during the Holocaust. But they also have a proud history of coming together, fighting back against discrimination, and celebrating their culture and religion as a community.

> For LGBTQ+ people of faith, it is important to find religious communities that embrace them, such as Reform Judaism, Unitarian Universalism, the United Church of Christ, and most pagan groups.

Equality is important within a religion, too. There are many examples of religions treating their members unequally based on gender, race, sexual orientation, or other features. Many faith groups prevent women from being leaders, for example. Some people react to discrimination in their religion by deciding to leave that religion. They may decide that another religion, or no religion, is better for them. Others decide to protest by working with other members of their religion to help change that religion and make it more inclusive.

GLOSSARY

ADHD a condition some people have, which means they may have some problems with the way their brain works compared with other people. These problems can include finding it hard to concentrate, focus, or sit still, having a lot of energy, and doing things quickly without thinking.

ANXIETY a feeling of worry or nervousness. We all experience anxiety sometimes, but for some people it can be a problem nearly all the time.

AUSTERITY when governments try to save money by spending less on wages, public services such as schools and hospitals, benefits such as help for disabled people or those on low pay, and schemes to help poorer people in society.

AUTISM a range of ways in which someone's brain works differently from other people's. Autistic people may find it difficult to communicate or to understand other people's feelings, and they may be distressed by loud noises, bright lights, or unfamiliar situations.

CATHOLIC someone who belongs to the Catholic church. Catholics make up one main branch of Christianity.

CIVIL RIGHTS people's right to be treated as equal and protected by the law.

COLONIALISM when one country claims the right to rule over another country and its people.

CONSTITUTION a formal set of rules that sets out how a country works, how its government operates and what rights its people have.

DEPRESSION an illness in which a person feels very sad and hopeless most of the time for a long time.

DYSLEXIA a condition in which someone's brain works differently from other people's, so that it can be difficult to see or read words easily—the letters may appear jumbled up or as if they won't stay still.

EXPLOITED used in a way that is unfair to the person being used. For example, a worker who is exploited may not be given a fair wage for what they do, or may be made to work in unsafe conditions.

GENOCIDE the deliberate killing of a large group of people, especially those from a particular group, in an attempt to get rid of them altogether.

HOLOCAUST the name for the deliberate killing of six million Jewish people and millions of others by the Nazi regime during World War II.

IMMIGRANT someone who comes to live permanently in a country, from another country.

INCLUSIVE set up in a way that means everyone can be included and no one is left out.

INDIGENOUS a word used to describe people who have lived in a region since before people from another part of the world first arrived. Examples include Native American and First Nations peoples in the USA and Canada, and Aboriginal Australians in Australia.

INTERNMENT CAMP a prison camp that holds people from a certain group, for example citizens of an enemy country during wartime.

JIM CROW LAWS racist laws that meant Black and white people in the Southern states of the USA were segregated (separated)—with Black people having fewer rights and opportunities and poorer access to education, housing, and more—from the 1870s to 1968.

KU KLUX KLAN a racist, white-supremacist terrorist organization in the USA. It opposes civil rights for Black people in particular and also Jews, LGBTQ+ people, and many other ethnic, religious, and social groups. It does this through very violent acts such as attacking and killing Black people.

LGBTQ+ a term used for several groups of people with different sexualities and genders. The L is for "lesbian"— a girl who is attracted to other girls; G is for "gay," which usually means a boy who is attracted to boys, although sometimes lesbians use this term for themselves too; B is for "bisexual," which means someone who is attracted to boys and girls, or can mean attraction to at least two genders (such as to girls and non-binary people). T is for "transgender" (see definition below) and Q is for "queer," which can mean different things to different people, but generally applies to anyone who isn't heterosexual or "straight" (a girl attracted to boys or vice versa). The plus sign is another way of representing anyone who isn't straight.

NAZI a member of the group that ruled Germany from 1933 to 1945. Nazis did not respect human rights and saw Germans as superior to everyone else. They started World War II and carried out acts of extreme cruelty, especially the Holocaust.

NEURODIVERSITY the range of different ways people's brains work. Often, people whose brains work differently from most people are called neurodiverse, but actually we are all neurodiverse! But some people have particular needs and characteristics because of the way their brains work.

NONBINARY someone who doesn't think of themselves as male or female—they may feel like they are a blend of both, or that they are neither.

OPPRESSED treated unfairly or cruelly, usually over a period of time and in an official way.

PREJUDICE judging a person or a group of people without getting to know them first, because of things you have read or seen or beliefs you hold.

PRIVILEGED having wealth or other advantages such as a good education, good health, or simply being a member of a favored group, such as white people or men.

PROTESTANT someone who belongs to a Protestant church. There are many different groups of Protestants and together they make up one main branch of Christianity.

PSYCHIATRIST a doctor who treats mental illness.

PURITAN a member of a particular group of Protestants in the 16th and 17th centuries. Puritans wanted to reform the church and were known for their strict and solemn rules about how religious people should live their lives.

SCHIZOPHRENIA a serious mental illness in which a problem with the brain means someone has strange thoughts or feelings that are not based in reality.

SEGREGATED separated. It especially refers to groups of people being officially separated by law, so that they are forced to live in different places, attend different schools, and have different resources, for example.

SEXUAL HARASSMENT annoying, upsetting, or bullying someone in a sexual way.

SLAVERY when people are treated as if they are the property of their bosses, forced to work in terrible conditions, for little or no pay, and with no say over what they do. In the USA, for example, Black people were kept as slaves from the 17th century to 1865. Slavery still exists today, even though laws aim to prevent it.

STEREOTYPE when people wrongly think that someone from a particular group will behave in a particular way, or that certain things are appropriate for that person or not. For example, it is a stereotype that girls cry more than boys, or that Black people are naturally better at some sports than others.

TRADE UNION a group of workers who formally join together to push for improvements on things like pay and safety.

TRAIT another word for a feature, quality, or characteristic.

TRANSGENDER someone whose gender is different from the sex they were assigned at birth.

TRANSPHOBIA hatred or discrimination against transgender people.

UN (UNITED NATIONS) a group of many countries that work together to prevent and end wars and also to protect people's rights and improve people's lives all around the world.

WORKING CLASS can mean anyone who must work in order to survive, as they don't have other wealth, and are not rich or powerful. Usually it means a narrower group of people who do certain jobs including physical work or care work, which often don't pay a lot. Examples include factory workers, builders, bus drivers, postal workers, shop assistants, cleaners, waitstaff, hairdressers, and caregivers.

INDEX

A
ableism 18, 20
accessibility rights 20
apartheid 26, 27
austerity 36
autism 18, 19

B
beauty myths 12
birth control 15
Black Lives Matter 30–31
boycotts 35

C
Chávez, César 35
classism 32–33
colorism 28
consent 14, 15
Copeny, Amariyanna "Mari" (Little Miss Flint) 29

D
disability 18–21, 27
diversity 17, 31, 44
double standards 7

E
economic justice 11
education 4, 5, 8, 11, 15, 32, 33, 36, 41, 45
environmental racism 29
equality: what it is 4–5, 30
equality of opportunity 33
eugenics 27

F
families 14, 17, 24, 33
feminism 8–9, 11, 12, 15

G
gender 6–7, 8, 9, 14
gender stereotypes 7, 9

H
hate crimes 42
healthcare, access to 20, 32
Holocaust 27, 45
homophobia 14, 16, 17, 21
Huerta, Dolores 35
Hutchinson, Anne 43

I
immigrants and refugees 34, 40–41
  see also migrants

J
Johnson, Asean 23

K
Kahlo, Frida 21

L
labor activism 34–36
LGBTQ+ people 8, 14, 16–17, 27, 45

M
male privilege 9
Mandela, Nelson 26, 27
mental illness 19
migrants 25, 35, 36, 39

N
nationalism 38, 41
neurodiversity 18, 19
non-binary people 6

O
Obama, Barack 29, 35

P
Pankhurst, Emmeline 8
politicians 9, 10, 26, 27
poverty 10, 11, 20, 25, 32, 40
privilege 4, 9, 22, 28, 33

R
racial profiling 30
racism 22–31, 38, 40, 41
religion, freedom of 42–45
religious discrimination 45, 49
religious pluralism 44
reproductive freedom 8, 15

S
Scholl, Sophie 38
segregation, racial 24, 26
settler colonialism 41
sexism 6, 7, 10, 12, 21, 33

sexual equality 14, 16–17
sexual orientation 14, 16
sexuality 14–15
skin bleaching 28
slavery 24–25
stereotypes 7, 9, 30, 39
suffragettes 8

T
Thunberg, Greta 19
trade unions 34–35, 36
transgender 6, 14
transphobia 14, 16

V
voting 8

W
white privilege 9, 22, 28
white supremacy 23, 26, 27, 28, 31
women and girls, rights of 8, 9, 10–13
workers 11, 32, 33, 34–36

X
xenophobia 39, 40, 41

Y
Yousafzai, Malala 11

48

DISCUSSION TIME

Write a list of all the chores that have to be done in your household—by you and your siblings, by your parents or caregivers, and anyone who comes in to help out.

Who does the chores, and are they shared equally by people of different genders?

Do you think this is fair?

If not, what changes would you like to make?

Can you give an example of a mean stereotype used against a group and a way members of that group prove the stereotype wrong?

How might you be able to show your friends and neighbors from a different racial group that you care about them and their safety?

50

Can you think of examples of xenophobia you've read about in history or that are happening today? What are some ways we can help make members of our communities who may have moved here from somewhere else feel more welcome?

Have you ever heard or seen someone (including yourself) being treated differently for their religion or lack of religion? How do you think it made them feel?

Can you think of examples of people working for equality in your community, country, or the wider world?

Think of a public spot that is often used in your community, such as a library, park, or beach. In what ways is it accessible for disabled people? In what ways could it be more accessible?

When we talk about sexuality, why do you think consent is one of the most important things to understand and practice?

What are some ways you've experienced classism, or seen classism used to discriminate against others? In what ways would our world be different if everyone was born into a family where they had plenty of money? How might we make such a world a reality?

In what ways do you have privilege, and in what ways do you and/or your family face discrimination?

QUIZ

1. Before the 1940s, little boys were often dressed in what color?

a) blue
b) orange
c) pink
d) green

2. Which of these women was a famous English suffragette?

a) Susan B. Anthony
b) Elizabeth Cady Stanton
c) Emily Murphy
d) Emmeline Pankhurst

3. Which country made Sanna Marin prime minister in 2019?

a) Denmark
b) Finland
c) Brazil
d) Canada

4. Malala won the Nobel Peace Prize for campaigning for girls' right to what?

a) education
b) the vote
c) better healthcare
d) free meals

5. Who designed the LGBTQ+ rainbow flag?

a) Gilbert Baker
b) Brenda Howard
c) Harvey Milk
d) Marsha P. Johnson

6. Which of these is NOT an example of neurodiversity?

a) ADHD
b) dyslexia
c) deafness
d) autism

7. Which of these famous artists was disabled?

a) Vincent Van Gogh
b) Frida Kahlo
c) Henri Matisse
d) Michelangelo

8. Martin Luther King, Jr. led a march to which city in 1963?

a) Chicago
b) New York
c) Los Angeles
d) Washington

9. "Little Miss Flint" protests against what environmental problem in her home city?

a) air pollution
b) poisoned water
c) a new oil pipeline
d) trees being destroyed

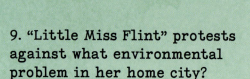

11. Who was the first Black president of South Africa?

a) Nelson Mandela
b) Barack Obama
c) Paul Boateng
d) Kofi Annan

10. What movement did Patrice Cullors, Alicia Garza, and Opal Tometi start in 2013?

a) HeForShe
b) Black Lives Matter
c) School Strike for Climate
d) Never Again

12. César Chávez and Dolores Huerta led a strike of thousands of what kind of workers?

a) factory workers
b) farm workers
c) nurses
d) teachers

Answers: 1c, 2d (the others were famous suffragists in the US and Canada), 3b, 4a, 5a (the others were also important LGBTQ+ activists in the 1960s and 1970s), 6c, 7 all of them (trick question! Frida Kahlo is featured in this book, but the others worked despite their disabilities too), 8d, 9b (but the others are examples of environmental racism in other places), 10b (the rest are other activist movements started in the 2010s), 11a (the rest were also the first Black person in a particular top job), 12b.

56

FIND OUT

- What are the top ten languages spoken in your country or city?

- Write down all the different national cuisines represented by restaurants in your neighborhood or your nearest town.

- Who is your senator, state representative, or other government official?

- What are the five most common religions in your country? (Lack of religion may be in the top five.)

- Ask a family member if you have any relatives or ancestors who were immigrants or refugees, or who were subjected to settler colonialism or enslavement. What is one question you'd like to ask that person about their life?

- Go online and look up your city or town to see if there are any protests planned for the near future. What is/are the protest or protests about?

Which activist in this book would you most like to find out more about? Do some research of your own and write about them in the space here. You can draw a picture, if you like!

GET ACTIVE

What are your hopes and dreams for a more equal world?

What three things would you do to try and make your society more equal?

How would you do it?

Activist actions

VOLUNTEER! Pick an organization that works for equality or helps marginalized groups, and find out what you can do to support them.

WRITE A LETTER! If you see an example of inequality happening, find out who has the power to make it better (a politician, the head of a company, your school principal) and write to them. Write your request clearly and respectfully. .

START A PETITION! This is like writing a letter, but you tell lots of people about it and persuade them to sign it, too. You can gather signatures on a physical letter on paper, or set up an online petition.

HOLD A FUNDRAISER! Why not hold a bake sale, sponsored bike ride, or concert to raise money for a cause you care about.

COMMUNITY ACTION: it's not just about money! Many organizations that help marginalized groups welcome other kinds of donations. For example, charities that help refugees or victims of gender-based violence often need donations of food, clothing, books, and toys.

BUY FAIRLY! Try to become aware of how the things you buy are made. Do the companies that make them treat people fairly, or are they contributing to modern slavery or environmental racism, for example? You can choose to buy things produced fairly, or boycott things that make inequality worse.

Be an ally

Allyship is kind of like friendship. It means that when there is a type of oppression or discrimination that doesn't target you (like racism if you're white, or sexism if you're male), you stop, listen, and believe the experiences of the people who do experience it. You make sure to educate yourself—such as by reading this book!—and you figure out the actions you can take to make the world equal alongside those who don't have the privilege(s) you do. Some ways to be an ally include:

- Think about and change the language you use.

- Stand up to discriminatory comments and actions, including things that people with privilege pretend are "just jokes." Make sure you stick up for those who don't share your privilege even when they're not in the room.

- Follow the leadership of the people who are being discriminated against—don't assume you know what's best for them.

- But don't expect marginalized friends to teach you about how to take action; they are likely tired from having to deal with discrimination in their daily lives. Instead, learn from the resources that are already out there (books, films, podcasts, speeches at protests, and more).

- Remember that being discriminated against in one or more ways doesn't mean you can't have privilege in other ways. For example, a white gay man may experience homophobia, but he also has white privilege and male privilege. Each of those three things matters.

- Educate your friends and family who share your privilege on how that privilege is harmful to those without it and how you can work together to make things more equal.

Remember that there is always more to learn. You are never done becoming an ally!

Take inspiration

Look back at the examples of kid activists in the book and what they did to fight for equality. Can you think of something similar that you could do?

WRITING and DRAWING ACTIVITIES

Use this space to design a poster for an equality cause important to you (Black Lives Matter, Love is Love, Girls Can Do Anything, etc).

Be an artist for equality! Draw a picture representing what an equal, just society would look like. Where would people live? What would their daily life look like? What would be different compared to the neighborhood you see around you now? Create it!

Think about all the superhero films you have seen or stories you know. Are they diverse? Are the heroes of different genders, different races, and do some of them have disabilities? Do they represent you?

Try your hand at writing a superhero story in which the hero is like you, or is like someone else you'd like to see in a central role.

Write a poem about why equality is important to you and why activism matters.

63

> Write a news report about an example of inequality you have seen on TV recently. Make sure it includes the views of the marginalized people in the story. (These can be imaginary for your report, but a real reporter should always make sure they interview people and get their views for real!)